STACY MILLS

CHRISTMAS IN SPAIN

How to Enjoy a Traditional Spanish Navidad

Christmas in Spain : How to Enjoy a Traditional Spanish Navidad

Stacy Mills

Published by Stacy Mills, 2024.

CHRISTMAS IN SPAIN : HOW TO ENJOY A TRADITIONAL SPANISH NAVIDAD

First edition. October 3, 2024.

Copyright © 2024 Stacy Mills.

ISBN: 979-8227209962

Written by Stacy Mills.

Also by Stacy Mills

The Strategic Christmas Planner : Christmas Made Simple
Christmas in San Francisco : Love, Magic, and Miracles by the Bay
The Christmas Vegetarian : A Vegetarian's Guide to a Meat Free Christmas
Christmas Cash Flow : Proven Strategies for Holiday Financial Success
Noel in Germany : How to Celebrate the Holidays like a True Local
The Smart Holiday Planner : Budgeting for a Merry Christmas
German Christmas Shopping : A Shopper's Wonderland
Christmas in Spain : How to Enjoy a Traditional Spanish Navidad

Table of Contents

INTRODUCTION... 1

CHAPTER 1 | THE SPIRIT OF SPANISH NAVIDAD.......................... 5

The Enchanting Streets and Festive Atmosphere................................... 9

The Role of Family and Tradition 12

CHAPTER 2 | MADRID'S FESTIVE MAGIC 15

Exploring the Mercado de Navidad in Plaza Mayor............................. 19

Street Performances and Festive Treats 22

CHAPTER 3 | FESTIVE TRADITIONS AND CUSTOMS................... 25

The Excitement of El Gordo Lottery 29

Nochebuena—The Heartwarming Christmas Eve Feast 33

CHAPTER 4 | CULINARY DELIGHTS OF THE SEASON 36

Traditional Christmas Dishes and Sweet Treats 40

Drinks and Desserts that Define Spanish Navidad 44

CHAPTER 5 | CELEBRATIONS BEYOND CHRISTMAS DAY........ 47

The Three Kings Parade: A Grand Spectacle... 50

The Significance of Epiphany and the Festivities.................................. 54

CHAPTER 6 | THE ART OF THE NATIVITY 58

The Belén—A Showcase of Craftsmanship.. 62

Live Nativity Scenes and Community Spirit.. 65

SUMMARY 69

INTRODUCTION

E nter a world where every sparkling light, every joyful grin, and every mouthwatering taste brings the spirit of Christmas to life. Spain's holiday season is an opportunity to discover the charm of a custom rooted in history, culture, and the coziness of a community, rather than just a time for celebration. Imagine yourself meandering through sparklingly lit cobblestone streets, the aroma of roasted chestnuts filling the air, and the sound of laughter resonating from busy plazas. This is Spanish Navidad, a Christmas unlike any other, with tales to be told around every corner.

Forget about the hectic Christmas madness you may know. Spain reinterprets the meaning of the season. In this place, Christmas is a time for communities to gather together, celebrate tradition, and exchange gifts. It's a festival of the senses. Imagine yourself in the middle of Madrid at a holiday market, where the aromas of freshly made pastries and hot cocoa mingle while craftsmen sell their handcrafted wares, each of which embodies a unique aspect of Spanish culture. The authentic Christmas spirit is revealed in these lively marketplaces, beckoning you to partake in something timeless and enchanting.

Every town and city in the nation lends a unique touch to the Christmas festivities. There's a tangible sense of happiness and community everywhere you look, from the magnificent Three Kings Parade through the congested streets, to the little family feasts on Nochebuena. One of the most eagerly awaited events of the season is the parade, which is known locally as "Cabalgata de Reyes." Unlike other regions of the world that wind down after Christmas Day, Spain maintains the festive atmosphere alive long into January. Both adults and children wait in line, their eyes wide with excitement as the Three Kings walk by, throwing candy and bringing joy to all. It's an occasion that perfectly encapsulates the wonder and possibility that come with childhood.

Spanish Christmas rituals are incredibly distinctive and represent the deeply held beliefs and customs of the nation. This is the time of year when the new and the old meet, and every location has its own unique celebrations. Picture the vibrant streets of Seville, where the vibrant costumes of the flamenco dancers twirl in the sparkling lights, evoking a dynamic atmosphere. Imagine instead the sleepy, peaceful towns of Galicia, where families huddle around warm bonfires to tell tales that have been passed down through the ages. This variety, this blending of lavish metropolis displays and small-town get-togethers, is what makes Christmas in Spain so very special.

Without food, a Spanish Navidad wouldn't be complete, and this is the time of year when Spain's gastronomic customs are most apparent. The holidays are a feast for the senses, from the spicy smells of roasted lamb and seafood delicacies to the sweet taste of turrón, a nougat that's been loved since the period of the Moors. On "Nochebuena," or Christmas Eve, families get together for a feast that is more than just food. It's an occasion to celebrate cultural heritage and foods that unite people via telling historical tales. There's the warmth of a shared table full of love and laughter, the sound of corks bursting as bottles of cava are opened, and the distinct aroma of saffron in a paella made especially for the occasion.

El Gordo, Spain's famous Christmas lottery, is another highlight of the festive season. It is more than simply a chance game; it is a national tradition. Families, friends, and even complete strangers gather on December 22nd to hear the draw. Today is full with anticipation, optimism, and a feeling of untapped potential. It's the experience that counts, regardless of the outcome. It's about feeling like you're a part of something bigger, about the happiness that comes from feeling the thrill and anticipation together. El Gordo serves as a reminder of the ability of tradition to unite people in a world when the holidays can sometimes feel commercialized and disengaged.

But the small things are just as important as the major occasions when it comes to what makes Christmas in Spain unique. It's the peaceful beauty of a nativity scene, or "Belén," lovingly made and displayed in a town square or a family's living room. These nativity scenes are artworks that vividly depict the Christmas story; they are more than just decorations. Some are straightforward, with only a few figures, while others are intricate, with whole villages with miniature shepherds, glittering stars, and flowing rivers. Every single one is an expression of love and an homage to the caring and giving spirit of the season.

Spain's streets are alive with music, from spontaneous street musicians performances to customary carols. It's not unusual to see gatherings of people singing under the stars, their voices rising in unison. Contagious excitement and spontaneity permeate the atmosphere, serving as a reminder of the true meaning of the holidays. Music has a vital role in Spanish Christmas celebrations, whether it be a street corner performance by friends or a choir in a huge cathedral.

A fundamental component of Spanish Navidad is community. It's clear from the way people congregate in plazas, from the meals that are shared to the group celebrations that characterize the season. There's a feeling of inclusivity that permeates the celebrations, transcending the boundaries of specific families. Christmas in Spain is a time to celebrate family and community, from large parades to the straightforward act of eating dinner together. It's about being a member of a community that extends an open hand to everyone, sharing in the happiness of others, and opening your heart.

Spain's Christmas celebrations will make you feel at home even if you're distant from home. Everyone is welcome to join in the celebrations because of the warmth, friendliness, and genuine excitement that permeate the air. You'll experience the beauty of the season every step of the way, whether you're wandering through streets decked with lights, taking in a seasonal delicacy at a holiday market, or watching the Three Kings Parade.

This book serves as your guide to fully enjoying Christmastime in Spain, with all of its wonder and beauty. It's a welcome to a world where custom, neighborhood, and festivity all join together to make something genuinely unique. This tour will teach you how to celebrate the holidays like a real native, whether your goal is to travel to Spain for the holidays or you just want to add a little bit of Spanish Christmas cheer to your own house. In Spain, Christmas is a time to celebrate joy, warmth, and the charm of family time, whether it is in the huge parades or the quiet country towns, in the vibrant markets of Madrid or the cozy family meals.

CHAPTER 1
THE SPIRIT OF SPANISH NAVIDAD

Spanish Navidad is a burst of color, love, and enduring tradition. It's the kind of magic that wraps around you the instant you step onto the cobbled streets, with a light winter breeze carrying the aroma of freshly roasted chestnuts and churros soaked in thick, velvety hot chocolate. During these holiday weeks, which are a time of genuine community, every corner is transformed into a show of lights, laughing, and the reassuring bustle of people getting together.

As the center of the celebration, Madrid takes the lead. The yearly Christmas market at Plaza Mayor turns into a hub for both locals and tourists. Beautifully carved ornaments, nativity figurines, and other Christmas items are sold by artisans beneath the market's blazing kiosks. The centuries-old masonry of the plaza is reflected in the lights of the market, creating a nostalgic, celebratory, and altogether enthralling ambiance. Madrid's excitement sets the standard for the entire nation as it is the capital city. The market is alive with the excitement of families browsing the busy aisles, folks striking up a conversation, and the distinctive sound of children laughing—the sound of the holidays.

Another vital component of the Spanish Christmas celebration is the "El Gordo" lottery. Given that it is the world's largest lottery in terms of both prize money and tradition, its name, "the Fat One," fits it perfectly. Every home gathers around radios, TVs, and these days, cellphones on December 22nd, listening carefully as schoolchildren sing the winning numbers in a chorus that reverberates across coffee shops, living rooms, and offices. The thrill is in the shared excitement more than the jackpot victory. Colleagues, neighbors, and family purchase tickets collectively, sharing the expense and possibly the benefit. As the numbers are recited one by one, a sense of unifying hope is created within the community. Beyond money, the custom transforms into a rite that unites everyone.

Nochebuena, or Christmas Eve, is very important in Spain. With candles blazing against platters of traditional dishes, families congregate around long, exquisitely arranged tables. One of the most significant events of the year is this evening feast, when the aromas of saffron, garlic, and rosemary fill the house and family members reminisce. Platters of jamón Ibérico and shellfish delicacies like gambas al ajillo usually surround the roasted lamb, or "cordero asado," which usually takes center stage. Every recipe has a backstory and is handed down from grandmother to grandchild, with each ingredient chosen with care. The dessert table is never complete without turrón, a honey and almond nougat that is a throwback to Spain's Moorish history, and polvorones, which are crumbly cookies that melt in your mouth and leave a deep almond flavor behind.

Songs float through the air as the feast comes to an end. Around the table, carols, or "villancicos," are sung to the sound of tambourines and laughing. These tunes have a timeless quality to them, reflecting the diverse history of Spain shaped over ages by the blending of various areas and cultures. The music of Navidad is rich in history, ranging from the lively Renaissance carol "Riu Riu Chiu" to regional folk tunes. It unites families in a common display of happiness and crosses generations with well-known songs.

Another beloved custom begins at midnight with "La Misa del Gallo," or the Mass of the Rooster, which gets its name from the rooster that is said to have crowed the night Jesus was born. Candlelight softly illuminates the faces of worshippers as churches fill with people. The air in these old stone structures is heavy with incense, and hymns resound from the lofty ceilings. The togetherness of people gathering in the quiet of midnight to celebrate peace, optimism, and regeneration is deeply affecting, and even nonreligious individuals can't help but feel reverence for one another.

The start of a new year brings with it its own traditions. Spanish people have a custom of eating twelve grapes at midnight, one for each chime of the clock, in hopes of good fortune the next year. Laughing as they try to keep up, families and friends huddled in front of television broadcasts from Madrid's Puerta del Sol frequently burst into grins as their cheeks swell with grapes. It's a simple but significant ceremony that stands for hope, community, and the conviction that every day can be better.

Nativity scenes, or "Belén," have special positions in houses. Some of these enormous pieces of art, which occupy entire rooms and feature small villages, rivers, and intricate landscapes depicting not just the nativity but also daily life in Bethlehem, are not your ordinary nativity sets. Impressive displays can be found in churches and public areas. Some towns even offer live nativity reenactments, which feature singers, farm animals, and locals dressed in medieval costumes. The devotion to these exhibitions is evident in the meticulous arrangement of each figure, which not only depicts a biblical story but also the community's inventiveness and passion.

And then comes January 5th, the eve of Epiphany, when the enthusiasm reaches its zenith with the "Cabalgata de Reyes," or the Three Kings Parade. The streets of Spain come alive with lights, colors, and music during this time. Melchior, Gaspar, and Balthazar, the Three Kings, make their appearance on ornate floats and give candy to children who are giddy with anticipation. Words can barely express the enchantment that permeates the atmosphere. Children burst into giggles as they rush to collect as many candies as they can, and parents hoist small children over their shoulders for a closer look. It serves as a reminder that the holiday season is a time for generosity, kindness, and joy in addition to celebrating the gifts that were given to the infant Jesus. Even on the coldest nights, the parade brings warmth and a sense of awe to all, which lasts long after the floats have gone by.

When youngsters wake up on January 6th, they discover gifts from the Three Kings. Overflowing with gifts, shoes are set out on balconies or windowsills the night before, and the day is filled with joyous play. Once more, families gather to celebrate by sharing a "Roscón de Reyes," a ring-shaped cake adorned with candied fruits. A little figurine of a king and a dried bean are hidden within the cake; the one who discovers the king wins the day's crown, while the person who finds the bean is stuck having to pay for the Roscón the following year. It's a fun custom that involves competitiveness and lots of laughing.

There is a constant sense of community throughout the season. Spanish Navidad is not observed in private; rather, it is experienced in public settings such as plazas, streets, shared dinners, and open-to-all festivities. The celebrations are given a special liveliness by street musicians, spontaneous dances, and flamenco performances. The deep, heartfelt notes of flamenco mix with the brilliant lights and the aroma of food in the air of Andalusia. The season has a distinct flavor that is unique to each place, yet connection, tradition, and joy are always there at its core.

These few weeks serve as a reminder of what really important. The spirit of Spanish Navidad is captured in the lights that line every street, the family lunches, and the delight of children seeing the Three Kings. It's a celebration centered on warmth, community, and the centuries-old rich fabric of tradition rather than on extravagance or excess. The essence of Spanish Navidad is found in its capacity to transform each moment into a shared gift that binds individuals to one another, to their past, and to the profoundly basic delight of being in each other's company.

The Enchanting Streets and Festive Atmosphere

The festive mood hits you like a warm hug the instant you set foot on Spain's cobblestone streets during the Christmas season. There is a captivating ambiance that entices you in, with streets bursting with color, laughing emanating from the intimate cafes, and sparkling lights adorning every structure. Every town and city has a tale to tell, combining customs and culture to create a tapestry that elevates the commonplace to the spectacular.

The air is filled with the delicious fragrances of seasonal delights as festive decorations line the roads in Madrid, the capital of Spain. Renowned Plaza Mayor comes to life as a lively marketplace with the sounds of both locals and visitors chatting. Vendors provide artisan ornaments, one-of-a-kind presents, and delicious delicacies that entice the palate. Everywhere you go, there are sweet delights like turrón, a classic nougat made with honey and almonds. Take a bite, enjoy the crispiness, and allow the sweetness to dance across your tongue.

The strains of Christmas carols reverberate as you walk around the streets, bringing happiness and nostalgia into the atmosphere. Local musicians congregate in plazas where their tunes intermingle with the chuckles of friends and family. Around every turn is another joyful display, such as a children's choir performing touching melodies or a band of musicians playing classic Spanish tunes that beckon you to join in the fun. The vibrancy of the streets is like a heartbeat that echoes the mood of the season.

The charming streets come alive in the evening. Above you, strings of lights glitter like stars, illuminating the night sky and fostering a surreal atmosphere. Vendors offering this festive treat will entice you with the aroma of roasting chestnuts. Warm your hands around a paper cone full with these nutty treats, and savor in their smokey, sweet flavor while you continue your journey.

When exploring the communities, you'll find that each has a distinct charm and festive flair of its own. Vibrant paintings and unique stores in the Malasaña district provide as a backdrop for the festive mayhem. Young people congregate at hip cafés, where they share tales of their holiday plans and customs while savoring creamy hot chocolate. The contagious energy makes you feel like a member of the group and a participant in the season's collective joy.

Towns like Seville and Granada in Andalusia, which is further south, captivate your heart with its elegance. Orange tree-lined streets sparkle with lights, and belenes—traditional nativity scenes—decorate homes and public places. With finely detailed figurines and well placed details, every exhibit tells a narrative. These scenes arouse curiosity as they beautifully and artistically portray faith and tradition by bridging the past and present.

The neighborhood markets, or mercadillos, burst to life as the holidays approach, presenting a variety of handmade products, colorful decorations, and delectable delicacies. Talk with craftspeople as they relate their tales, from the beginnings of their trade to the meaning behind their works. Every encounter personalizes your experience and serves as a reminder of Spain's rich cultural legacy, which sets it apart as a tourist destination.

The markets are only one place where the lively atmosphere spills over into the neighborhoods as residents enjoy holidays with friends and family. Wreaths and garlands cover balconies, and sounds of conversation and laughing waft into the streets. Families get together for small dinners with traditional fare as dusk draws near, fostering a feeling of coziness and friendship that begs you to join in. The rich flavors of Spanish cuisine come alive as roasted lamb, seafood paella, and robust stews decorate the tables, complemented by clinking glasses filled with sparkling cider or wine.

Every meal becomes a festival, a reminder of the joy of sharing food and laughs with loved ones. The tables are laden with festive fare, each morsel representing the local cuisine. An alluring invitation to join in the feast is created by the aroma of fresh ingredients and spices mingling in the air.

The joy of the holidays keeps showing itself as you stray farther. To commemorate the advent of the Magi, families and friends gather in the streets for the Three Kings Parade, or Cabalgata de Reyes, in early January. A vibrant mood is created by animated music, colorful floats, and happy kids while candies descend from above. This magnificent show turns the streets into a lively celebration of joy and solidarity, capturing the spirit of community and tradition.

Everything about life is filled with celebration, and the warmth of the season is reflected in even the smallest of interactions. Shopkeepers greet you with genuine enthusiasm, baristas smile and pour steaming mugs of coffee, and strangers exchange joyful greetings, their faces lighting up with the joy of the holidays. Every moment is unique because of this sense of connectedness, which creates a story of belonging and community that cuts over barriers of language and culture.

Spain's streets welcome you with a festive atmosphere as the days become shorter and the nights get colder. With every step comes a new experience, a new custom, and a fresh link to a culture that fervently embraces life. Enjoy a celebration of love, family, and togetherness that lasts long after the last lights go out on the charming streets, which are alive with the sights, sounds, and tastes of the season.

There's a distinct thrill in the air, a rush that marks the advent of a season where time slows down, and the basic joys of life take center stage. Every moment spent strolling through the festive streets of Spain provides a window into a world where Christmas is more than simply a day, but rather a season full of magic and wonder, a chance to rediscover what really matters. From the sparkling lights that light your way to the mouthwatering aromas that dance on your tongue.

Participating in the customs and festivities enables you to be a part of something far greater—a vibrant, dynamic culture that embraces all people. The charming streets and festive ambiance provide a space where memories are built, laughter is exchanged, and the spirit of Christmas shines brightly, igniting every heart that walks through.

The Role of Family and Tradition

F amily get-togethers over the holidays weave a colorful tapestry of happiness, coziness, and shared memories in Spain. Every household turns into a center of activity and excitement come Christmastime. Every family has its own customs that are frequently passed down through the centuries, giving each celebration a special flavor that combines old and new memories. Youngsters look forward to the celebrations with great anticipation, and grandparents tell tales of past Christmases filled with love and laughter.

Nochebuena, which takes place on December 24th, is the focal point of the celebration, when family gather to share a feast that goes beyond simple nourishment. It's a gastronomic adventure full with cherished recipes that every family has developed over time. Succulent paellas, shellfish, and roasted lamb set the setting for a visually stunning feast. The aroma of spices fills the air, and the sound of glasses clinking as toasts are raised to celebrate the family connection as much as the feast.

Candy is a major component in these celebrations. Sweet nougat called turrón becomes a beloved centerpiece over the holidays. Made with sugar, honey, and almonds, it has a history that illustrates the various cultures that have influenced Spain. Every mouthful is exploding with taste, taking everyone back to those decadent dinner table memories from years past. Crumbly almond cookies called polvorones, when combined with turrón, melt in your tongue and make you feel cozy and in love.

Apart from the delectable cuisine, the customs related to exchanging gifts underscore the profound bonds among relatives. During the celebration of Reyes Magos on January 6th, many families exchange gifts instead of exchanging gifts in a frenzy on Christmas morning. Children wait in anticipation for the arrival of the Three Wise Men, who customarily bring gifts. The idea that the season is more about connection than materialism is reinforced by this activity, which fosters a sense of enthusiasm and solidarity. Waiting creates anticipation and helps families focus on what really counts: quality time spent together.

Stories come to life and laughter fills the air when family members get together around the table. Every family talks about their unique holiday customs, which frequently sparks fun arguments about the tastiest recipes and timeless tales. In this way, the holiday dinner becomes a vibrant celebration that intertwines a highly personal and distinctively Spanish story for each family. These shared experiences, which range from embarrassing incidents to youthful pranks, form an integral part of family life.

Traditional music frequently fills the air, bringing delight to the gathering. Families may break into song, voices harmonizing as well-known carols ring out. Everybody is drawn into the spirit of the season by the contagious energy that festive music creates as it reverberates through homes. Music unites families and spans decades as they join in harmony, whether it's a new take on a classic song or a traditional villancico.

During the holidays, Spanish families typically stress the value of community. It is typical for friends and neighbors to join in the celebrations, obfuscating the distinctions between community and family. Open doors encourage generosity and compassion by welcoming people who are in need. Christmas encourages everyone to embrace a sense of connection that goes beyond conventional borders, even if they are not part of a family.

Families frequently participate in a variety of activities that deepen their bonds as the Christmas season progresses. Baking becomes a family favorite, bringing generations together in the kitchen to create delicious delicacies. The kitchen turns into a place of laughing, flour, and the delicious smell of baked products. Together, hands of all ages produce mouthwatering treats and lasting memories that are created long after the final cookie is consumed.

Making nativity scenes, or "Belénes," is another popular pastime. Families take great pleasure in building these elaborate displays, frequently adding personal elements that correspond to their own tales. Some people draw intricate pictures that include persons from their personal life in addition to the Holy Family. Youngsters get involved with great enthusiasm, discovering the customs that have molded their families and creating bonds with their roots. When the nativity scenes are finished, they become the center of attention in the house, encouraging everyone to take a moment to consider the real meaning of the season.

In Spain, the main themes of Christmas celebration are love, community, and togetherness. It's a time when families set aside their everyday routines to appreciate the delight of being with one another. The spirit of tradition spreads across them like a warm blanket as they assemble around the table to share meals, tales, and laughs. Every second spent together becomes a thread sewn into the tapestry of family history, guaranteeing the longevity of these treasured memories.

Different regions have different traditions, creating a rich tapestry of customs that every family adds to. For example, the "Caga Tió" in Catalonia gives the holiday celebrations a lighthearted touch. This painted-face wood becomes the focal point of family get-togethers. Kids alternately beat the log with sticks while humming classic tunes until it "poops" out gifts. This beautiful ritual emphasizes the value of playfulness and innovation within family customs while bringing laughter and joy.

In the Basque Country, families gather for a sumptuous Christmas lunch with unique regional cuisine. Here, the festivities transform into a multisensory affair that combines delectable food with the comforting intimacy of told tales. With the tastes that have graced their tables for years, each bite holds a history that unites generations. The Basques place a strong focus on community, which includes eating meals together to strengthen ties and make enduring memories.

Family becomes the center of the Christmas season when viewed through the colorful prism of Spanish customs. Every get-together, dinner, and tale told illustrates the love that unites them, leaving a legacy that will last for generations. Families create ties during celebrations that last a lifetime, reminding each member of their position in the vast fabric of history and culture. These are the times when Christmas really comes to life and serve as a lovely reminder of what it means to belong.

CHAPTER 2
MADRID'S FESTIVE MAGIC

During the Christmas season, Madrid becomes a magical place where every street, square, and corner is alive with charm and celebration. Excitement permeates the air as happy noises of laughter and tantalizing smells from food vendors fill the air. When you go about the city, you can't help but get caught up in the festive mood as bright lights shine overhead, illuminating the busy streets below.

Plaza Mayor is where the beating center of Madrid's Christmas festivities is located. This beautiful architecturally framed historic square serves as a focal point for festive pleasure. Along the cobblestone walkways are stalls offering a variety of goods, such as delectable seasonal fare and handcrafted ornaments. Guests can peruse a variety of distinctive presents, each capturing the spirit of Spanish culture. A warm, rich hot chocolate invites you to linger and enjoy the tastes of the season, making it the ideal beverage for dipping churros. Locals and visitors mix together in this place, weaving together a colorful tapestry of voices and laughter as they all enjoy the festivities.

Madrid's famous lights come to life as evening descends. Every street in the city is illuminated by the brilliant display, creating a breathtaking spectacle. Known as the Spanish Broadway, the Gran Vía is adorned with an amazing variety of decorations. The city is alive with vitality, from the spectacular window displays to the glittering stars hanging overhead. A charming ambiance that begs for unhurried strolls is created by each storefront appearing to vie for the attention of onlookers. The whole city seems to get involved in the festivities, shrouded in a sense of coziness and amazement.

A mouthwatering selection of culinary treats is available in the Christmas markets. The aroma of roasted chestnuts permeates the air alongside the handcrafted goods, luring onlookers to indulge in regional delights. Try the delicious nougat called turrón, which is made from almonds and honey, or the flaky, melt-in-your-mouth almond cookies known as polvorones. The flavors that have been passed down through the centuries allow each bite to tell a story and link the past to the present. When you're standing next to a market stall, you might hear lively Spanish-language discussions, laughter that melts into the sounds of cooking food, and an overall enticing atmosphere that pulls you in.

Madrid holds the well-known "El Gordo" lottery in December, a national holiday. Families congregate around televisions on December 22nd, with excitement growing with each number that is shown. Everyone participates in this cherished custom, from young children to elderly folks, in the hopes of sharing in the happiness that comes with winning. As friends and families gather to watch the draw take place, the day turns into a national holiday, bringing joy and laughter to many neighborhood cafés. This custom brings a special sense of camaraderie to Madrid, bringing the city's residents closer together over the holidays.

Nochebuena, or Christmas Eve, is a time when families prepare for one of the most important feasts of the year, and the warmth of the occasion falls over the city. Tables creak beneath the weight of classic foods, each morsel brimming with cultural significance. The main course is roast lamb, which is served with seafood dishes that pay homage to Spain's maritime history. Families get together to laugh and tell stories, making enduring memories. As the evening wears on, it's typical to witness loved ones raising glasses of cava and raising a toast to good health, joy, and unity. As the evening draws in, the streets are filled with a festive vibe that is accentuated by the sound of laughter and singing.

A fitting conclusion to the holiday season is the January 5th "Cabalgata de Reyes," or Three Kings Parade. Vibrant floats with actors dressed like the Three Wise Men pass through the streets. Children's laughter blends with the music played by marching bands as they reach out for the candies dropped from the floats, their eyes filled with wonder. The vivid display captivates viewers, guaranteeing that the festive mood endures well after Christmas Day. The procession invites families to join together one last time before the decorations are taken down, symbolizing the pinnacle of the Christmas season.

The "Belén" tradition, which involves creating a nativity scene with extraordinary care, is widely observed throughout the city. In homes and public squares, numerous families euphorically showcase scenes from the Christmas tale on their Belénes. Some go even beyond, building intricate dioramas that feature whole villages and small miniatures portraying everyday life. People walking by are drawn to these elaborate works of art and stop to admire the artistry. Youngsters especially take pleasure in identifying their favorite characters from the figurines, which helps them feel more connected to their culture and the meaning of the holiday.

Madrid's cathedrals, with their exquisitely decorated altars and facades, also exude a festive charm. Christmas Eve Midnight Mass attracts a large number of residents, who fill the air with the sounds of prayers and hymns. In the middle of the season's enthusiasm, the occasion's seriousness offers a chance for introspection. Every historically significant church has a distinct atmosphere and welcomes those who want to experience the religious aspect of the occasion.

There are also a lot of cultural activities going on during this time of year. Theaters are showing Christmas productions that perfectly embody the spirit of the season. Flamenco shows, replete with vivid costumes and passionate dancing, offer a genuine touch to the festivities. Attendees' hearts are touched by the performances' rhythm and vigor, which fosters connections via a love of art and joy.

Madrid shows itself as a place where tradition and modernity coexist together as the season progresses. An exciting atmosphere is created by combining traditional rituals with modern festivities, enticing everyone to partake in the fun. By incorporating their unique style, local artists and performers make every encounter feel interesting and novel. A live music event in a plaza or a pop-up Christmas market are two examples of events that constantly take place, providing an occasion to get together and celebrate.

Madrid is brimming with bustle in the days before Christmas, an unmistakable energy emanating from every angle. An contagious happiness is created by streets crowded with merchants, families gathered in parks, and friends enjoying meals together. Every interaction is permeated with the spirit of the holidays, reminding everyone who comes that this time of year is about community, connection, and shared joy.

Every second spent in Madrid over the Christmas season embodies the essence of the holiday. From the great parades to quiet family meals, the city delivers a unique blend of sensations that remain long after the last ornament is taken down. Madrid's holiday magic turns this energetic city into a joyous, traditional, and warm refuge that welcomes everyone who wants to enjoy the splendor of Spanish Navidad.

Exploring the Mercado de Navidad in Plaza Mayor

As December approaches, the heartbeat of Madrid intensifies with enthusiasm. Plaza Mayor's Mercado de Navidad turns the ancient square into a colorful wonderland that embodies the sights, sounds, and smells of a classic Spanish Christmas. This vibrant market, which has mesmerized tourists for centuries, acts as a focal point for both locals and visitors who are ready to get into the festive spirit.

While strolling through the market, one may hear friends and family chatting, their voices blending with the joyful music coming from adjacent booths. The area is lined with vibrant wooden booths, all decked out in nostalgic holiday décor and sparkling lights. The vendors display a variety of handcrafted goods, from delicate ornaments to artisanal crafts, with cheery grins and inviting gestures. There is a chance to find one-of-a-kind items that showcase Spain's rich cultural legacy around every turn.

Sweet delights scream out from food stands, tempting customers to savor the season's sweet flavors. A rich perfume of roasted chestnuts fills the air, blending with the sweet aroma of candied fruits and the enticing smell of freshly fried churros. For those looking for a warm and comfortable escape from the cold winter air, steaming hot chocolate in thick mugs is ready. Language difficulties don't stop locals from dipping their churros into the chocolate for a moment of pure joy.

Apart from the delicious food and handicrafts, the market exudes a sense of community. Gathering around stalls, families exchange stories and savor seasonal goodies while laughter reverberates. Youngsters point out nativity decorations and figures with excitement, their eyes glistening with curiosity. Warmth permeates the air, reminding everyone that the holidays are about more than just presents—they're also about the happiness of spending time with loved ones and making enduring memories.

There is a thriving level of craftsmanship in the market. Artists take great delight in the work they do, showcasing the passion and effort that goes into each creation. The market provides a window into the skills and customs that characterize Spanish culture, showcasing anything from exquisite hand-painted ornaments to exquisitely built wooden nativity scenes. Every object has a backstory that reflects the traditional knowledge that has been passed down over the ages. Conversations on the meaning of the customs the craftsmen preserve and the inspiration for their products are frequently held between visitors and craftspeople.

The market comes alive as dusk draws in under a canopy of sparkling lights. The illumination gives the joyous atmosphere a magical touch and entices onlookers to stay a little longer and appreciate the occasion a little more. The air is filled with the sounds of music and laughing, and periodically, performers appear to share festive songs that uplift the atmosphere even further. Everyone is surrounded by a sense of celebration and community, which forges an enduring sense of shared belonging.

Finding interesting things while meandering through the market turns into a fun journey. Whether it's choosing a box of turrón to go home, trying out some locally made cheeses, or choosing a lovely handmade ornament, every station offers a unique experience. Selecting gifts turns into a happy journey that immerses guests in the essence of Spanish customs. The colorful decorations all around them serve as inspiration for anyone looking to create their own festive ambiance at home.

Visiting the Mercado de Navidad offers an additional opportunity to become familiar with Spanish holiday traditions. Having cordial conversations or shared laughs with the locals might provide greater understanding of the significance of different customs. The warmth and hospitality of the Spanish people create a welcoming environment, where conversations flow readily and friendships are created amidst the festivities.

Even in the busy atmosphere, there are quiet moments. Amid the bustle of the market, finding a quiet place to sit encourages contemplation of the basic pleasures of the season. There is a tangible sense of unity that is created when one witnesses family interactions, friend smiles, and youngster giggling. It becomes evident that this holiday season goes beyond personal festivities and serves as a universal reminder of the value of family and community among people from all walks of life.

The Mercado de Navidad serves as a reminder to give as Christmas gets closer. Here, presents have a deeper meaning than money; they are symbols of affection and thoughtfulness. Whether it's a delicious delicacy or a handcrafted object, choosing the ideal gift for a loved one becomes a significant ritual. It's all about encapsulating the spirit of the season and fostering giving delight in a neighborhood gathering spot.

Modern celebrations blend with festive customs throughout the market. The fusion of the old and the new is a reflection of Spain's dynamic culture, in which traditional traditions coexist with modern celebrations of the holiday season. A vibrant atmosphere that promotes exploration and engagement in the diverse array of Spanish Christmas customs is created by this harmonic balance.

The market in the center of Madrid continues to be a source of happiness and light as the evening wears on. Warmth and anticipation enter hearts as time goes on, strengthening the bond with the holiday spirit. Long after guests have left, the beauty of Plaza Mayor's Mercado de Navidad lingers, bringing back memories of jubilant celebration of an incredibly amazing season, laughing, and camaraderie.

It's important to stop, breathe, and notice the beauty around you in the middle of all the bustle. The sensory experience that embodies the spirit of Spanish Navidad is created by the brilliant colors, joyful melodies, and delicious seasonal food. Engaging with the local culture, enjoying the warmth of community, and indulging in wonderful delicacies create a tapestry of memories that endure long after the holiday season ends.

This market is a celebration of life, love, and the spirit of Christmas rather than merely a place to shop. Every visit enhances the enjoyment of the customs that distinguish Spanish Christmas, enabling visitors to take away not just a few mementos but also a portion of the happiness and coziness that permeates the atmosphere.

Street Performances and Festive Treats

The colorful streets of Spain come alive with festive delights that entice the senses and performers who bring life to every corner as the holiday season approaches. Every plaza is alive with the sounds of music blending with the delectable scents emanating from neighboring vendors, as well as laughter and conversation. This joyous environment is enhanced by street acts, which make even the most mundane stroll into an amazing experience.

Dancers and musicians enliven the scene with their passion in places like Madrid and Barcelona. Flamenco dancers whirl around, dazzling onlookers with their flair and deft movement as flamenco guitarists play their tunes. The streets are alive with the sounds of musicians strumming guitars, people clapping their hands rhythmically, and singers' powerful voices, which entices both locals and tourists. Every show conveys a tale while capturing the happiness, grief, and rich cultural diversity that characterize the Spanish people. For a moment, all else goes away, leaving only the music and the shared sense of joy.

During the holidays, the Plaza Mayor in the center of Madrid comes alive. Performers from diverse backgrounds assemble here to enthrall the audiences. Aerial jugglers hurl vibrant balls into the air, and magicians enthrall spectators with devious feats. There is a distinct sense of enthusiasm and color added to the environment with each performance. When a clown dances, kids squeal in excitement, and adults stop to admire the unplanned humor and inventiveness that's being displayed. The square transforms into a mingling pot of laughing, cheers, and cultures—a miniature version of the greater celebration taking place all around the city.

And there are the snacks, the sweets, the sweets! A tempting blend of scents wafts through the air as each street seller provides a delicious treat. A corner booth offers warm, sugar-dusted churros that are great for dipping in a cup of rich hot chocolate. Each bite's crunch perfectly complements the chocolate's creamy richness to create a decadent experience that uplifts the spirit. Gathering around vendors, families enjoy sharing a box of turrón, the delicious nougat made with honey and almonds. Taste receptors are transported to a land of seasonal pleasure by this delectable delight, which is sometimes laced with tastes like orange or chocolate.

Another classic holiday favorite are the crumbly, melt-in-your-mouth almond cookies known as polvorones. These treats are wherever you look, their aromatic aroma blending with the clear winter air. A polvorón tastes like embracing a part of Spanish ancestry when you bite into one. Every crumb brings back memories spanning several generations, speaking of get-togethers with family and laughing around a table. Merchants frequently divulge family-secret recipes that have been passed down through the generations, giving a unique touch that enhances the experience.

It becomes different when night falls. Warm, golden light filled the streets as the festive lights flickered to life, lighting the artists and their audiences. Artists join the stage, showcasing both contemporary hits and classic carols, fusing genres to create a welcoming celebration for everybody. As spectators sway to the beat, lost in the moment, groups of friends congregate, singing and dancing to the beat. The happiness is contagious and cuts over linguistic and cultural divides.

The atmosphere of the holidays also inspires original performances that echo the themes of the season. You may come across nativity scene reenactments—miniature dramas that illustrate the birth of Jesus—during these weeks. With a heartfelt performance, local troupes invite the audience to partake in the celebration of family and life. Youngsters frequently take on important parts, assuming the roles of angels and shepherds and showing obvious joy at being included in the narrative. When family and friends come together to see the wonders of Christmas come to life, these performances foster a feeling of community.

Mantecados are a must-try for anyone looking for a delicious treat that perfectly captures the spirit of the occasion. Made with flour, sugar, and nuts, these classic cookies are delicious and melt in your mouth. Vendors cook them in a variety of flavors, such as lemon, chocolate, and cinnamon, each of which reflects the diverse culinary traditions of Spain. A beloved Christmas tradition is splitting a box of mantecados with loved ones; it's a straightforward gesture that strengthens bonds and happiness.

Street performances and festive snacks weave together the fabric of Christmas celebrations across Spain. They foster friendship and fun by bringing people together, and the delicious smells of holiday treats make everyone feel at home. While adults relish the moment and think back to previous holiday seasons, children skip through the streets, their eyes filled with amazement. Every experience, whether it's the delight of watching a passionate flamenco dancer perform, the suspense of watching a magician perform, or the pure joy of tasting a freshly cooked churro, becomes a treasured memory that is inextricably linked to the spirit of Spanish Christmas.

Feel the warmth of the holiday atmosphere as you walk through the streets that are lit up. Come enjoy the performances, laugh with the masses, and savor the foods that make this holiday season so memorable. Every step brings a fresh discovery, whether it's a new melody, taste, or relationship. Beyond simple enjoyment, the experience captures the essence of Spanish culture, where joy, community, and tradition combine to produce something very amazing.

CHAPTER 3
FESTIVE TRADITIONS AND CUSTOMS

The holiday season in Spain is marked by a vibrant array of traditions and practices that weave together to create a rich and vibrant environment. Both locals and tourists are enthralled by the vibrant colors, aromas, and flavors that erupt from every corner of the nation. Every area lends a special touch to the festivities, creating a colorful and endearing ethnic mosaic. Christmas is all about community and shared experiences, from busy markets to family get-togethers.

The first thing that strikes you when you go through the streets during this festive season is the variety of decorations that turn even the most mundane plazas into enchanted wonderlands. Buildings are decked with twinkling lights, and spectacular displays attract people in by creating a cozy atmosphere. The sounds of music, laughter, and the joyful commotion of holiday shoppers fill the air. A variety of seasonal sweets are sold by street sellers, luring onlookers to partake in the flavors of the moment.

After a downpour, holiday markets appear like mushrooms, transforming squares into quaint wonderlands full of stalls bursting with handcrafted goods, delectable pastries, and traditional ornaments. The Mercado de Navidad in Plaza Mayor is a must-see in cities like Madrid. Here, craftspeople showcase their handmade items, such as exquisite "Belénes," or nativity scenes, which artistically portray the birth of Christ. With minute details that highlight the skill of regional craftspeople, each figure in the nativity scene tells a unique tale, bringing history and culture to life.

There is a flutter of excitement and anticipation in the air as families get together for Nochebuena, or Christmas Eve. This is no average dinner. Gathering around the table to share stories, laughter, and an abundance of delectable dishes, this feast unites generations. A mix of seafood delights and a saffron-infused paella that fills the room with enticing scents support the main course of roasted lamb. During the lunch, food serves as a medium for fostering relationships as people bond over cherished recipes that have been passed down through the years.

Many families participate in the custom of going to Midnight Mass, or "La Misa del Gallo," after the feast. The lovely ceremony begins when the church bells ring. The faces of people present to commemorate the birth of Christ are illuminated by the flickering candles in the low light. Everyone in attendance feels a sense of unity as a result of the reverence and excitement that permeate the atmosphere.

An additional element of excitement to the holiday season is provided by El Gordo, the fabled Christmas lottery. Families gather around televisions on December 22 to watch the results with much anticipation. This yearly occasion, rich in history dating back to 1812, represents the spirit of optimism and community rather than just being an opportunity to earn money. The triumphant yells of the victorious ripple across the streets, bringing communities together as families rejoice in their newfound good fortune. The lottery unites people in a common experience that surpasses personal luck and brings happiness to the entire neighborhood.

After Christmas, people celebrate Three Kings' Day, or "Día de Reyes," on January 6, which carries on the celebratory spirit. Spain celebrates this event in particular because it commemorates the coming of the Wise Men with presents for the infant Jesus. Parades light up the streets, replete with colorful floats, music, and performers dressed as the Kings themselves. As candy drops from the floats, children throng the sidewalks, their eyes wide with expectancy. Everyone participates in the festivities on this magical and wonder-filled day, from the youngest to the elderly.

A much-loved ritual during this time is the Three Kings' Day "Roscón de Reyes," a classic cake. The round pastry, decorated like a crown with candied fruits, is a delicious snack to be enjoyed with loved ones. There are surprises within the cake, usually a dried bean and a figure. The finder of the bean has to purchase the roscón for the next year, but the finder of the figurine gets to be king or queen for the day. Every mouthful becomes a thrilling mystery as a result of this amusing ritual that infuses the celebration with excitement.

During the holidays, music is a major factor in fostering interpersonal relationships. The celebratory ambiance is further enhanced by the sound of carousers singing traditional tunes that reverberate across the streets. It's not unusual to see families or groups of friends getting together in town squares and singing their favorite holiday songs. Flamenco music frequently sets the mood, providing a lively background for impromptu dance parties. Everyone is brought together by the music's beat, which inspires them to have fun and enjoy the celebrations.

Additionally, customs differ by region, with each contributing its own special flavor to the festivities. The humorous tradition known as the "Caga Tió," or "Log of Poop," originated in Catalonia and embodies the spirit of Christmas fun. In the living area sits a wooden log with a painted face and a traditional cap on it. Children tend to the log in the lead-up to Christmas, giving it snacks and singing to it. The log is then struck with sticks while singing on Christmas Day, and after some joyous prodding, it "poops" out toys and candies for the kids. This fun custom highlights the festive mood of the season by bringing happiness and laughter.

Towns and cities also conduct a plethora of festivals and activities throughout the day to commemorate the rich fabric of Spanish culture. The intricate nativity scenes in the "Belén" displays, which travel to different places, are nothing short of works of art. The grandiose displays that local communities put up are a source of pride for them; they frequently portray entire towns or villages with minute details that put spectators right into the heart of the Christmas tale. Visitors can spend hours enjoying the craftsmanship and inventiveness, appreciating the artistry that goes into each scene.

Every ritual on this joyous trip emphasizes the importance of community. Neighbors join together to engage in local events, whether it's a communal meal, a concert, or a charity drive. The spirit of giving is woven into the fabric of Christmas in Spain, as people reach out to those in need, representing the essence of compassion and solidarity. Local markets act as hubs where locals come together to share commodities, laughs, and stories as well as to build a sense of community.

During this time of year, culinary traditions are also quite important. Apart from the celebratory meals, windows of bakeries are adorned with seasonal sweets, tempting onlookers with their pleasant scents. Mantecados, a sort of shortbread, and polvorones, crumbly almond cookies, become festive favorites. These sweets are commonly made by families together, strengthening bonds via common baking experiences. The wonderful aroma of freshly baked products and laughter flood the kitchen, which turns into a center of activity.

Spain's holiday customs continue to produce priceless memories with each day that passes. Every gathering, every meal, every song performed vibrates with the spirit of joy. Everyone is reminded of what really matters at this unique time of year—connection, community, and the shared joy of gathering together to celebrate life and love—by the warmth and excitement that pervade the air. Every custom invites everyone to share in the joy of the season by acting as a thread connecting the past and present.

The Excitement of El Gordo Lottery

The thrill surrounding the El Gordo lottery turns Spain's Christmas season into an unforgettable event that transcends simple chance. Each year, this much-anticipated occasion attracts family, friends, and even strangers together, creating a palpable stir in every corner of the country. The excitement in the air thickens as December approaches. Although there are decorations all over the streets, the real show is on December 22nd when millions of excited eyes turn to television screens and the air is charged with anticipation.

With its origins in 1812, El Gordo's history further heightens its allure. This lottery is more than simply an opportunity to win; it's a custom rooted in optimism, camaraderie, and common goals. Sales of tickets begin in July, and by the time Christmas draws near, excitement is building. The air is filled with the sound of youngsters performing the customary draw at Madrid's Teatro Real, a vibrant show that turns the occasion into a national holiday. These children, who are frequently from a nearby school, recite the winning numbers in a happy, catchy chant that reverberates across the country. This happy show is the culmination of a group journey that brings everyone together in excitement.

Even though the tickets might run up to 200 euros, many people can afford them since they are available in décimos, or tenth shares. Even if sharing a ticket with friends or family might spread happiness and bring people closer together, a single ticket has the potential to lead to a life-changing event. Buying a décimo is common among local groups, and each little donation turns it into a ray of optimism. Cheers and yells of joy break out throughout houses, cafés, and streets when the winning numbers are eventually revealed. People laugh and cry together as they celebrate, and for many, the true gift is that sense of togetherness.

The days before the lottery unroll in El Gordo, as the town develops its own distinct rhythm. Coffee shops turn into hive centers of activity as people talk about who bought tickets, how many décimos they bought, and what they planned to do with their winnings. It's not just about the money; it's also about aspirations and opportunities, trip itinerary ideas, new residences, and even presents for close ones. The conversations unite the country as they construct a tapestry of desire and optimism.

Neighbors congregate in the streets to share their lottery hopes as the frenzy erupts. Shops report a spike in customers searching for lucky charms to add to their festive mood, while cafés are bursting with conversation. The common anticipation acts as a unifying factor, elevating the ordinary into something exceptional, whether in little towns or thriving metropolises. Shops put up their own décimos, with each ticket serving as a sign of the community's unity as they imagine what winning might mean for their establishments and families.

As the big day draws nearer, families start getting ready for the festivities. Those who have had the good fortune to win in the past frequently share their tales with their loved ones, igniting hopes and desires in them. People congregate for substantial feasts full of customary foods and celebratory treats, and food becomes an essential component of the festivities. The chatter flows as freely as the laughter, with turrón and polvorones taking center stage and creating an ambiance that perfectly captures the essence of the season.

Everybody is on high alert the day of the draw. As friends and family check in with one another, homes fill with the sounds of laughing, clinking drinks, and the inevitable buzzing of phones. As everyone watches the event live, local get-togethers start. As the audience holds its breath in anticipation of each number being picked, there is an infectious energy that permeates the auditorium, accompanied by exclamations of excitement or dejected looks. Everybody leans in closer to the TV, hearts pounding with hope, as the draw is televised live. The children sing the numbers.

The memories that El Gordo evokes are just as beautiful as the possible winnings. Regardless matter the outcome, families rejoice and embrace the happiness that comes with being together. It turns into a pivotal point in the Christmas season, brimming with a spirit of unity that permeates every toast and conversation. The stories they tell, the dreams they dare to share, and the optimism that comes from being a part of something greater than themselves provide comfort to even those who come up short.

Although winning the lotto can change your life, the real magic happens in the minutes before the draw. Communities come together via the shared excitement, engaging discussions, and group energy in a way that lasts long after the final number is drawn. Talks about the winnings' potential impact on the future are common in the days that follow, which inspires hope and plans ranging from small-scale endeavors to exciting international travel.

The essence of El Gordo lingers throughout the Christmas season, permeating every aspect of the celebrations. Its happiness isn't limited to one day; it carries over into the New Year, bringing optimism and a sense of community to people's hearts. Communities come together through sharing hopes and anecdotes, reminding one another that there is more to the lottery than just winning money.

El Gordo serves as a potent reminder that, despite the commercialization of the holidays, what really counts are the relationships and shared experiences. This lottery's enthusiasm goes beyond just winning money; it's a celebration of community, optimism, and the allure of Spanish Christmas. People are still getting together, having meals together, and celebrating their relationships, which is the real spirit of the holidays. A common thread, a fabric of happiness and expectancy, the build-up to El Gordo makes every Spanish Christmas a memorable occasion that leaves a lasting impression on everyone who celebrate it.

Nochebuena—The Heartwarming Christmas Eve Feast

Every Christmas Eve, houses throughout Spain are transformed into lively centers of laughter and joy by the delightful Nochebuena feast. Families congregate in kitchens smelling of good food simmering on the stove as the sun sets and the streets start to get silent. This is more than just a supper this evening—it's a beloved custom with a rich history and a strong sense of community.

An intricate buffet with a delicious fusion of flavors and textures makes tables groan. The festive table is dominated by saffron-infused paella, luscious shellfish, and roasted lamb, with each bite telling a tale that has been passed down through the years. Recipes, which are sometimes kept confidential, attest to the devotion that goes into each dish. A particular position is given to turrón, a sort of nougat made from almonds and honey, its sweet flavor blending with the savory dishes. Melt-in-your-mouth almond biscuits, or crumbly polvorones, are the ideal way to round off this rich feast and entice everyone to indulge a little bit more.

Families assemble around the table and greet one other with hugs and kisses. Excitement is in the air as everyone looks forward to the delectable feast that lies ahead. Talks are easy, a mash-up of smiles and happy recollections, each dish igniting memories of previous festivities and the dear ones that are missed. As grandparents share tales of Nochebuena from their childhood, children listen expectantly, their eyes bright with curiosity. Each anecdote has a golden ribbon-like thread connecting them all to the past.

There is a tangible sense of anticipation in the air as midnight draws near. This is when many families celebrate their ancestors with a sincere recollection by participating in the custom of sharing a meal. Warmth permeates the space as the first toast, which is followed by glasses of sparkling cava or a deep red wine, honors the joy of being with family. The sound of glass clinking and the aroma of tasty food drifting from the kitchen mingle together to create the sound of cheers.

Main meals frequently showcase regional products and cooking methods, reflecting local customs. Fresh seafood is the main attraction in coastal regions, where meals like salted cod (bacalao) are served with plenty of garlic and olive oil. With flavors that enhance each bite, tender, succulent roast lamb or pork embodies the spirit of a robust Spanish Christmas. Every plate is an expression of love woven into the fabric of tradition, telling a tale of place and culture.

Even though the lunch is definitely the main attraction, Nochebuena is much more than that. Families often congregate in the living room following the feast, their tummies full and hearts full. They might start singing villancicos, or traditional carols, which fill the house with joy and warmth. Youngsters anticipate the Three Kings' arrival with great anticipation, their anticipation evident from their dreams of the gifts that would soon be presented. Everyone is engulfed in the spirit of Christmas right now, immersed in a generation-spanning common experience.

A variety of delicious desserts that entice the palate round up the evening. Families also frequently make fruitcake and marzipan, two delectable holiday desserts that are full of nostalgia and flavor, in addition to turrón and polvorones. Even the most full-bellied guests are tempted to indulge a little bit more by the pleasant scent of cinnamon and citrus that lingers in the air. Cake slices and thick enough hot chocolate to hold a spoon erect are served together, making for a cozy conclusion to an amazing evening.

Many families celebrate another cherished custom as midnight draws near: going to the midnight Mass, also referred to as the Rooster's Mass or La Misa del Gallo. This church ceremony, which celebrates Jesus' birth amid candles and singing, embodies the pure spirit of Christmas. Families put on their best clothes and dedicate their hearts and thoughts to the evening's significance. As the community comes together, the church is filled with the sound of a beautiful tapestry of voices and faith. As a group, they uphold the festive mood while reinforcing their ties to one another and their beliefs.

Families return home after the church ceremony to continue the celebrations. Hearts brim with happiness, gifts are traded, and laughter resounds throughout. Long after the celebrations are over, the sense of community creates a lasting sense of belonging. The spirit of Spanish Navidad is the same, but each family adds their own traditions to the elaborate tapestry, making it a celebration of love, family, and unity.

The walls of the house appear to reverberate with affection throughout the evening, enveloping everyone in a comforting hug. Everywhere you look is filled with the music of delight and delicate shadows created by the flickering candlelight. Nochebuena is more than just a meal—it's a celebration of the strength of tradition, family, and the times that bind them all together. It captures the essence of Spanish culture, in which sharing meals becomes a means of fostering relationships, memories are made at the dinner table, and the warmth of shared experiences feeds the spirit of Christmas.

CHAPTER 4
CULINARY DELIGHTS OF THE SEASON

In Spain, food becomes a major topic during the Christmas season, turning every get-together into a feast that entices the senses. Tables creak beneath the weight of customary fare, each dish a masterwork that embodies generations of cultural and familial history. Every region has recipes that are passed down from one generation to the next, bringing love and memories to every meal.

As Christmas Eve draws near, the story-telling tastes of the festive table begin to take shape. Across the nation, Nochebuena brings families together, transforming dinners into colorful celebrations of human connection. The focal point is perfectly seasoned roasted lamb that is flanked by platters of fresh seafood, emphasizing the maritime influences. A mainstay in many homes, the saffron-infused paella glistens with brilliant colors, inviting everyone to assemble around it. With every mouthful, you are whisked away to sun-kissed beaches, where the rich flavor of saffron and fresh ingredients combines with the sea breeze.

During the holidays, turrón, a sweet treat prepared with honey and almonds, makes a magnificent appearance that pleases both young and elderly. This nougat-like treat has centuries-old origins and is influenced by the Moors. Turrón, which comes in a variety of textures—from soft and chewy to crispy and hard—is frequently the ideal way to cap off a festive dinner. Families are united by the lovely moments that bond them together, as evidenced by the joy and nostalgia that fill the air as they unwrap these delectable squares.

And then there are the crumbly, melt-in-your-mouth almond cookies known as polvorones. These cookies, which are made with flour, sugar, ground almonds, and a touch of cinnamon, are a holiday mainstay. Every mouthful crumbles flawlessly, scattering bits of powdered sugar across lips and fingers. They stand for coziness, warmth, and the delight of spending a special moment with close ones. They are simply delicious, especially when accompanied by a glass of sweet Spanish wine or a warm cup of cocoa.

During the holidays, sipping hot chocolate that is thick enough to hold a spoon upright becomes a treasured tradition. Friends congregate around steaming mugs, dipping churros into the silky richness, in homes as well as cafés. Warming the body and soul, this simple pleasure symbolizes the festive mood. People enjoy this beautiful custom, which transcends decades, and laughter fills the air as they partake in it.

Moving beyond the conventional menu, Spain's different regions also add their own culinary flair to the table. Canelons, a delectable pasta dish made with leftover meats from the Nochebuena dinner, are a common addition to the celebratory feast in Catalonia, establishing a lovely link between the past and present. This recipe is a genuine celebration of flavor and ingenuity, showcasing the inventiveness of families that take leftovers and make them into something quite remarkable.

In the Basque Country, seafood reigns supreme, with a particular focus on fresh harvests from the Atlantic. Dishes like bacalao a la vizcaína, a salt cod stewed in a rich red pepper sauce, produce a symphony of tastes that sing of the sea. Gathering around platters of delicious treats, families enjoy every mouthful of the meal while exchanging anecdotes that add to its specialness.

The Three Kings arrive, bringing with them their customary roscón de Reyes—a delicious sweet bread fashioned like a crown and decorated with candied fruits—and the revelry continues. Enjoyed on January 6th, this feast is full of surprises and signifies the end of the holiday season. There are hidden gems inside, such a dried bean and a tiny figure. Finding the figurine brings good fortune, but finding the bean means you have to buy the roscón the next year. This amusing tradition adds an element of fun to the feast, ensuring that the festivities linger just a bit longer.

Spain's holiday cuisine is a real expression of the country's rich history and diversity, with each region contributing its own flavors and customs. Every dish offers a backstory, a recollection, and a chance to get together with loved ones. A joyous ambiance that captivates the senses is created by the laughter shared around the table, the clinking of glasses filled with fine Spanish wines, and the perfume of home-cooked dishes.

By engaging in these culinary customs, one might enter a world where every meal is an occasion for celebration. Fresh fruit and seasonal treats abound in local markets, beckoning tourists to immerse themselves in the vibrant culture of Spain. Every moment is a sensory extravaganza, from perusing stands brimming with vibrant fruits and veggies to tasting cured meats and handmade cheeses.

The sounds of sizzling pots, children laughing, and the sense of community fill the streets as the holiday season draws near. In order to ensure that no one is left out of the celebration, families embrace the spirit of giving by sharing their culinary creations with friends and neighbors. People from different backgrounds are brought together by food and are invited to partake in the happiness and coziness that come from a celebratory feast.

Whether gathered around a large table or having a modest dinner with loved ones, the gastronomic delights of the season encapsulate the heart of Spanish Navidad. In addition to providing nourishment for the body, the customs and flavors infuse the spirit with a feeling of love and belonging. This special fusion of cuisine, culture, and camaraderie makes for lifelong memories and elevates every holiday season to an outstanding occasion.

Traditional Christmas Dishes and Sweet Treats

In Spain, the dining table becomes the focal point of the festivities during the cheerful rush of the holiday season, with customary foods and confections serving as the centerpiece. Every dish narrates a tale, a multicolored tapestry crafted from generations of family customs and culinary legacy. Mealtimes become a treasured ritual throughout the holidays, with each bite infused with memories of past encounters, love, and warmth.

On many tables on Christmas Eve, or Nochebuena, there is roasted lamb. This meal is about more than just eating; it's about sharing. Gathering around the table, families relish the tender lamb that has been marinated in a mixture of spices, garlic, and aromatic herbs before being slow-roasted to absolute perfection. The flavor-bursting delicate beef is frequently served with dishes that showcase local specialties. Maybe a big helping of potatoes prepared the Spanish way, or a hefty serving of roasted veggies seasoned with olive oil. Each ingredient on the plate serves a purpose—bringing families together in a spirit of joy and thankfulness.

Seafood earns its deserved place as a holiday favorite as the meal is prepared. Fresh seafood, shellfish, and calamari dishes look especially good on celebratory tables in coastal areas. Filled with a variety of seafood and aromatic spices, paella is a star attraction, characterized by its vivid saffron hues. With every bite, customers are whisked away to the Mediterranean coast, where tastes dance together in harmony. The air is filled with the sound of laughing and stories as families get together to create treasured memories as fresh, sparkling Cava—the perfect match for the festivities—clinks in glasses.

Dessert arrives when the evening wears on and the sweets take center stage. A delicious selection of sweets awakens the Spanish sweet desire. Turrón, a nougat produced from almonds and honey, becomes a symbol of the season. Its chewy, thick texture melts in your mouth and brings back warm feelings and memories.

A common love of this sugary treat unites generations with each bite, carrying hints of history. Turrón has its roots in Moorish culture and is still a festive mainstay today. Some families make their own custom mixes by combining flavors and nuts that are representative of their own histories and traditions.

Crumbled almond pastries called polvorones give another delectable layer to the festive spread. These melt-in-your-mouth treats are typically served with hot cocoa or coffee, making for a cozy combination that promotes relaxed table talks. With a hint of cinnamon and a coating of powdered sugar, each bite reveals a delicate mix of tastes that bring back fond memories of time spent with loved ones.

Mantecados are another form of crumbly shortbread prepared with sugar, wheat, and lard that is available throughout the holiday season. These snacks, which are frequently flavored with spices or nuts, have a wonderful crunch that goes well with the softer textures of other sweets. The aromas of freshly baked sweets fill the air as guests savor these traditional treats, mingling with the laughter and stories that permeate the space.

In addition to these cherished classics, a visit to any Christmas market uncovers a treasure trove of seasonal delights. Exhibiting a diverse range of chocolates, marzipan figurines, and seasonal delicacies, each stall beckons you to discover a realm of taste and consistency. These marketplaces transform into a sensory extravaganza where noises, colors, and scents converge to enthrall guests in a joyful swirl of festive pleasure.

During the holidays, churros—long, crunchy pastries—make the ideal afternoon snack. They make the ideal combination that cheers the spirit when dipped in thick, creamy hot chocolate. Sweet treats are sold by street vendors, who make sure that everyone who passes by can enjoy this easy yet fulfilling treat. The process of exchanging churros inspires a sense of camaraderie, a reminder that the festive spirit feeds on connection.

In many places, distinctive regional foods that are a reflection of the local way of life may also be served at the festive table. For example, "Tortell de Reis," a classic cake filled with cream and topped with candied fruits, is found throughout Catalonia. This cake is typically shared with family and friends to commemorate the advent of the Three Kings. The celebration is made more exciting and surprising by the suspense of discovering the figurine concealed inside the cake.

On Nochebuena, as midnight draws near, a vibrant vibe permeates the space. Gathering around glasses of Cava or regional wines, the guests raise their glasses in salute to life, love, and tradition. The shared meal symbolizes the spirit of the season, which is the reunion with loved ones and the common heritage that unites them all.

The sweetness of the season lasts long after the holiday feast is over. Sharing candies and cookies over the holiday season is a custom that many families still follow. Remaining polvorones and turrón provide as a reason to get together, fostering warm and funny times.

A classic Spanish Christmas feast is magical not just because of the food, but also because of the memories it evokes. It's about the affection that goes into making every dish, the chuckles that are had at the dinner table, and the tales that are handed down through the years. Food in this colorful festival becomes more than just a means of subsistence; it becomes a symbol of solidarity, a means of honoring the past while welcoming the future.

Every mouthful exposes a link to heritage, tradition, and the core of family. In Spain, customs that depict happiness, love, and coziness are portrayed on the dinner table throughout the Christmas season. Every meal and dessert offered throughout the festivities serves as a reminder of what it really means to spend Christmas in the real Spain.

Drinks and Desserts that Define Spanish Navidad

In Spain, every meeting is infused with a festive spirit throughout the Christmas season, with beverages and desserts taking center stage. The table becomes a treasure trove of flavors when families and friends meet together, with every bite and sip resonating with centuries of history. Warmth comes from sharing stories over a glass of smooth hot chocolate; it's the ideal way to start an unforgettable evening.

In Spain, hot chocolate is not your typical tea or coffee. Instead, it's a thick, creamy liquid that envelops you in warmth. It goes well with churros, those delicious fried dough sticks that entice you to dip, soak, and savor. It's thick enough to hold a spoon in. Both young and old will experience pure ecstasy when dipping a churro into this delicious elixir. Families enjoy this indulgence together, a beautiful tradition that spans generations, and streets and cafes are alive with laughter.

Cava emerges when the festivities intensify. This sparkling wine, which is mostly made in Catalonia, gives the toast a celebratory glimmer. A time of togetherness, happiness, and expectation for the future is symbolized by raising a glass of cava, whether at a Nochebuena family get-together or a New Year's Eve celebration. It dances on the palate, bubbly, crisp, and invigorating, bringing joy and laughter. Cava comes in a wide range of flavors, from fruity to floral, so there's something to suit every palate.

Spain offers great wine for individuals who want their wines with more complex flavors. For Christmas feasts, strong red wines such as those from La Rioja and Ribera del Duero provide a striking backdrop. Wine that is perfectly suited with savory foods like juicy lamb or tasty shellfish blends harmoniously together. Every drink improves the meal, making it more enjoyable and giving each bite more flavor. The pairing of food and drink creates a sense of community, whether you're sipping red wine and telling stories or sipping white wine and watching the lights twinkle.

During the holidays, desserts take center stage and create a delectable symphony of textures and flavors. Traditional Spanish nougat known as turrón is a popular holiday dessert. Made with almonds, honey, and egg whites, this treat has different textures—it can be soft or crunchy, and every bite has a satisfying crunch or chew. Turrón, which is typically consumed after a filling dinner, generates discussions and laughs that result in enduring memories at the table.

During the holidays, polvorones—those flaky almond cookies—have their own fan club. Everyone is welcome to savor these delicious treats that melt in your mouth. Gently crumbling each biscuit releases a wave of sweetness that dances across the mouth. Stories are told and laughing is heard when loved ones get together to savor these goodies, creating a mood that perfectly captures the spirit of the occasion.

During the Three Kings celebration, the Christmas cake, or "Roscón de Reyes," becomes a highlight. This circular cake doubles as a centerpiece and dessert. It is frequently decorated with vibrant candied fruits. Excitement is added with a secret surprise, such as a dry bean or a tiny figure. The finder of the bean has to purchase the Roscón for the next year, while the one who finds the figurine gets to be anointed king or queen for the day. This lively custom creates a sense of camaraderie and friendly competition among family and friends, reminding everyone of the joy of shared experiences.

Traditional flans, or natillas, are irresistible cream-colored custards that are a festive table staple. These desserts give a cozy conclusion to any dinner with their smooth textures and sweet flavors. Their understated elegance highlights the beauty of premium ingredients and tried-and-true recipes.

Throughout the holiday season, churros and chocolate, cava, turrón, polvorones, Roscón de Reyes, and creamy desserts form a tapestry of flavors that express the joy of celebration. Every beverage and dessert has a backstory that connects the past and present and beckons everyone to share in the coziness of community.

The desserts and drinks provide as a delectable reminder of the essence of the holidays, which is happiness, connection, and the beauty of shared experiences, as the celebrations progress. During the most joyful time of the year, every cava toast, every mouthful of turrón, and every chuckle over churros forms part of a beautiful story that honors the spirit of Spanish culture. Culinary customs come to life in an energetic setting, leaving a lasting impression and treasured memories for years to come.

CHAPTER 5

CELEBRATIONS BEYOND CHRISTMAS DAY

In Spain, the Christmas season spreads out its colorful strands well after December 25th, much like a vivid tapestry. After Christmas Day celebrations end, the festive mood changes to embrace a number of customs and occasions that prolong the cheer well into the New Year. Communities and families get together to make laugh-filled, delectable food-filled, and treasured memories.

In Catalonia, December 26th is celebrated as "El Día de San Esteban," a day for feasting and family get-togethers. Here, family gather to have a substantial lunch that frequently includes cannelloni filled with leftover meats from the previous day's feast, maintaining the joyful mood. Catalonia takes pride in its peculiar traditions, such the "caga tió," a comical log that children beat with sticks to encourage it into "pooping" out sweets. This lighthearted custom highlights the love of family that accompanies the season by bringing humor and enjoyment to the proceedings.

As January arrives on the calendar, the festivities continue. The main event is the magnificent "Cabalgata de Reyes," or Three Kings Parade, which takes place on January 5. Festive parades erupted in cities all around the country, with each float symbolizing one of the Three Wise Men: Melchor, Gaspar, and Balthazar. The streets are turned into a sea of color, music, and enthusiasm for this occasion. Families assemble in anticipation of the kings' arrival, when they fling candy and tiny presents to the happy kids below. The procession creates an ambiance of magic and expectation, bringing back that sense of wonder from childhood that frequently wanes with maturity.

The celebrations culminate on January 6th, which is known as "El Día de Reyes," or the Day of the Kings. In Spanish tradition, this day is extremely significant and frequently seen as more significant than Christmas itself. Families exchange gifts around this time, which is similar to what the Magi gave the infant Jesus. Breakfast is usually "Roscón de Reyes," a circular cake decorated with vibrant candied fruits that occasionally conceals a surprise figurine. The person who finds the bean has to purchase the Roscón for the following year, whereas finding the figurine portends good fortune for the upcoming year. The celebrations of the day get a little more exciting with this lighthearted touch.

As the season progresses, regional traditions become more prominent. Every Spanish region has its own distinctive festivals. For example, the "Carnaval" celebrations in Andalusia begin in late January or early February. Although it falls beyond the Christmas time, the essence of joy and festivity endures. Parades that honor life, culture, and creativity fill the streets, accompanied by colorful costumes and upbeat music. This blend of customs exemplifies Spain's multiculturalism, as one celebration blends into the next to produce a multifaceted cultural encounter.

The celebratory mood is further enhanced by the numerous fairs, festivals, and religious celebrations that take place throughout towns and cities during January. Tenerife celebrates the "Fiesta de la Candelaria" on February 2nd, honoring the Virgin of Candelaria with processions, music, and dance. This historic festivity embodies the enduring spirituality that permeates many of Spain's festivities. It's a reminder of the linkages between culture, tradition, and community, as family and friends gather together to recognize their ancestry.

Seasonal specialties take center stage in the culinary realm where festivities often make an appearance. Spanish tastes are emphasized in traditional foods made during this time, providing a sensory feast. Apart from Roscón de Reyes, tables all around the nation are adorned with filling stews, cozy soups, and delightful desserts. Recipes are passed down through families with pride, guaranteeing that the essence of community and sharing is ingrained in each and every meal. Cooking and eating these foods together creates a bonding experience full of stories, jokes, and treasured memories.

As January draws to an end, excitement for the forthcoming Carnival season starts to grow. Carnival celebrations turn the streets into a vibrant spectacle with parades, music, and spectacular costumes, especially in locations like Cadiz and Tenerife. This joyous occasion bids winter farewell and encourages people to welcome the next spring with open arms. Everyone is encouraged to participate in the fun and festivities that epitomize the Carnival spirit by the vibrant atmosphere.

Another important tradition is the June 24th celebration of San Juan, when bonfires light up the night to mark the arrival of summer. Families and friends gather to celebrate with music, dance, and a symbolic cleansing by jumping over the flames. This ceremony illustrates Spain's enduring customs that have their roots in antiquity.

Holidays aren't limited to December and January; they also extend into February with a variety of regional events. These events serve as a reminder of the value of family and community and the shared delight that characterizes Spanish culture. Every get-together, feast, and parade pays homage to the diverse range of Spanish customs that honor life in general and Christmas in particular.

With the approach of Easter, symbolized by Semana Santa, the celebrations continue as winter gives way to spring. Cities like Málaga and Seville come to life with solemn and joyful processions. Even though Semana Santa is a unique event, it fits in perfectly with the rest of the Spanish celebrations, serving as a constant reminder of the value of unity, culture, and religion.

The generosity and kindness that permeate the entire season serve to emphasize the importance of community. When neighbors get together, they share food, tales, and laughs, creating relationships that make people closer to one another. Beyond linguistic and cultural boundaries, the warmth of Spanish hospitality shines through, inviting everyone to enjoy the pleasures of the season.

The spirit of celebration lingers long beyond Christmas Day throughout all of Spain. The customs, rituals, and gatherings continue to construct a story of togetherness and joy. Families preserve their legacy by adding stories and memories that relive these unique moments to every year. The festivities offer a sincere invitation to share in life's joy and welcome each moment with open arms.

Spain teaches us the value of connections via all of its celebrations, including those with friends, family, and the rich customs that have shaped the country's culture. The bright parades, the warmth of shared feasts, and the echoes of laughter entice everyone to join in the colorful dance of life as the holiday spirit lingers. The celebration of joy, tradition, and community endures, leaving a legacy that spans generations and guarantees that the spirit of Christmas shines brightly all year long.

The Three Kings Parade: A Grand Spectacle

T he Three Kings Parade, or "Cabalgata de Reyes," is a spectacular event that culminates the Spanish Christmas season. Families and friends congregate in the streets on the evening of January 5th, and the atmosphere is electric with anticipation as children clutch bags to catch the candies thrown from grand floats, their eyes wide with wonder.

Cities and towns become vivid displays of color and light when night falls. Vibrant music and the steady beat of marching bands accompany the intricate floats that each represent one of the Three Wise Men: Melchior, Caspar, and Balthazar. The glisteningly decorated floats soar above the throng, which is frequently populated by happy children dancing and singing in bright costumes. The parade honors the Magi's journey, which they made to honor the baby Jesus, but in Spain it transforms into a beautiful celebration that enthralls people of all ages.

Eager to witness the sight, families are lining the streets. A lot of people show up early, claiming the best viewing locations, and frequently pack picnic blankets and refreshments to pass the time. Along with the sounds of laughing and conversation, the air is filled with the aroma of warm churros and roasted chestnuts. Parents create a sense of tradition that unites generations by telling their kids stories about the significance of the occasion. The spirit of the holidays in Spain is embodied in this coming together of the community and the sharing of space and spirit.

Festive music floats through the air as the parade starts, engulfing the throng in a euphoric atmosphere. As the monarchs, magnificent in their robes and crowns, wave to the happy children, colorful confetti showers down. The young viewers get into a frenzy as each king tosses miniature toys and sweets, signaling the pinnacle of enthusiasm. Shouts of happiness resound through the streets as kids rush to gather the sweet loot, their giggles blending with the applause of bystanders.

Not every float is simply about the monarchs, though; each one has its own story, frequently incorporating scenes from the Bible or aspects of Spanish mythology. Traditional music and dance are performed by local artists and dancers to complement the floats, adding to the spectacle. Musicians play upbeat rhythms that entice everyone to join in the celebration as flamenco dancers in vibrant costumes spin and stamp with enthusiasm. Every float in the parade adds to the epic story of the evening, making it flow like a river of happiness.

The procession acquires a certain regional flair in certain cities. Malaga's breathtaking fireworks light up the sky, bringing an added element of magic to the evening, while Barcelona's procession, featuring characters from Catalan folklore, winds through the streets like a bright tapestry. Every region has a unique perspective that highlights the wide range of cultures that make up Spain. them are united as the floats pass by, bringing them together through happy celebrations and common experiences.

The night sky turns into a rainbow of colors as the procession makes its way through the streets. A captivating glow was cast over the celebrations by the fireworks that burst overhead. With every explosion, the anticipation grows and lights up the faces of people below. Long after the last float passes by on the street, the atmosphere is heavy with the magic of the moment, leaving lasting memories.

The Three Kings' ghost lives on after the parade is over. When families get home, they're frequently gathering around the dinner table to celebrate with a special meal fit for the occasion. The star of the show is the spherical pastry called roscón de Reyes, which is filled with cream and adorned with candied fruits. Traditionally, the cake has a dried bean and a tiny figurine buried inside. Finding the figurine brings good fortune for the year, but finding the bean means having to purchase the Roscón the next year. This lighthearted custom brings a surprising and joyful touch to the festivities, serving as a constant reminder to everybody of the fun and friendship that characterize this unique time of year.

Communities come together to celebrate the Three Kings Parade, which highlights the virtues of joy, unity, and giving. Strangers bond over a shared custom that spans generations by grinning and laughing together. No matter where they are from, everyone feels linked in this setting because of the warmth of the festive spirit that permeates the air.

Children look forward to the arrival of the Three Kings, who are believed to bring gifts to those who have been good all year, in the days that follow the parade. A magnificent occasion arises on January 5th night when families place their shoes outside, stuffed with water and hay for the kings' camels. The excitement of discovery comes the next morning when kids wake up to discover gifts that have elevated the ordinary to the spectacular.

Witnessing the Three Kings Parade provides an insight into the core of Spanish society, where customs, happiness, and camaraderie come together. Everyone is invited to participate in the celebration, which perfectly encapsulates the spirit of the holidays. The procession not only signals the conclusion of the Christmas season but also establishes the framework for a year full of optimism, happiness, and the possibility of fresh starts.

Participating in this magnificent show turns spectators into participants, adding significance to every second. A memorable experience that stays with you is created by the vivid colors, upbeat music, and laughter. The Three Kings' spirit endures in this enchanted festival, serving as a constant reminder to all of the virtues of kindness, the strength of community, and the delight of gathering to commemorate life's special occasions.

The Significance of Epiphany and the Festivities

I n Spain, the coming of Epiphany, also known as the Three Kings Day, is a joyous occasion that brings excitement, expectation, and a plethora of colorful events to the end of the holiday season. Excitement fills the air on January 6th as friends and family get ready to celebrate the day that honors the Magi's visit to the Christ Child. Every town and city in the country is turned into a breathtaking display of warmth, color, and light on this day. It's a time when children's eyes shine with hope, and adults remember about their own childhood recollections of the celebrations.

Anxiety increases as daylight breaks. Families are busy getting ready as everyone looks forward to the Three Kings' visit. Children love placing their shoes by the window or beneath the Christmas tree, carrying out the custom of leaving them out the night before in the hopes of finding them packed with presents and surprises when they wake up. Snacks and sweets, typically a combination of cakes and cookies, are positioned close by, adding a touch of sweetness to the celebratory mood. As families join together, exchange memories, and transmit the stories of their own festivities, the act of preparing for the kings becomes a treasured occasion.

The true spectacle, however, happens in the evening, when the streets come alive with the legendary "Cabalgata de Reyes," the big Three Kings Parade. As colorful floats make their way through the crowds, this event fills the streets with laughter and joy. The floats are decorated with intricate decorations that bring the narrative of the Three Kings to life. These decorations frequently portray images from the Nativity or elements of Spanish culture. Families and kids are lining the streets, waiting for the parade to arrive with excitement in their hearts. The parade captures the spirit of Spanish culture and its passion of celebration with its kaleidoscope of colors, music, and performances.

Marching bands create a joyful environment by filling the air with upbeat melodies. Dancers in bright costumes move through the throng, enlivening and energizing the festivities. The streets are transformed into a sight right out of a storybook as the Kings themselves, dressed in regal regalia, wave to the cheering crowd. Children joyfully yell out their names, pleading with the kings to see them, while each float presents an own interpretation of the Kings and their gifts.

Children scurry to catch the candy as it flies in the air as it rains from the floats, creating a spectacular picture. Everyone is made happy by the contagious atmosphere of laughing and joy that permeates the streets. Laughing as they assist their kids in catching as many sweets as they can, parents frequently join in on the excitement. It serves as a lovely reminder that everyone is included in this celebration, strengthening the bonds of shared experience and community.

After the procession is over, the celebrations go on. Families get together for a festive lunch, and "Roscón de Reyes," a delectable ring-shaped cake adorned with candied fruits that represent the jewels in the kings' crowns, is frequently consumed. This cake hides mysteries within; buried inside are figurines and a bean. While finding the bean usually means having to purchase the Roscón the next year, finding the figurine is said to bring good luck. In addition to being enjoyable, this custom fosters camaraderie among those in attendance as they joke around and laugh together over who will find what.

Enjoying meals and desserts together turns into a moment to think back on the last few weeks of festivities and to welcome the promise of the next new year. Laughter and stories are shared during these times together, strengthening family ties. More than simply the food is involved in this occasion; it's about gathering to honor the depth of custom and the love that unites all people.

Beyond the festivities, Epiphany holds great significance. It acts as a reminder of kindness, charity, and the value of community. As the Magi's tale develops, it strikes a chord with principles of generosity and reciprocity, inspiring families to show one another their gratitude and admiration. People are encouraged to consider their blessings and to open their hearts to those in need by the general feeling of generosity that permeates the day.

People celebrate the significance of the monarchs' arrival by attending special services at nearby churches throughout the day. These rituals include social meetings, music, and prayer to fortify the bonds between friends and neighbors. The sound of the church bells heralds the beginning of this holy festival, during which families gather in thanksgiving and solidarity to uphold the principles of compassion and love that define the spirit of the occasion.

Candlelight flickers in windows around the nation as the sun sets on this enchanted day, signifying optimism and the coziness of community. Children's laughter hangs in the air, blending with the odors of home-cooked meals emanating from kitchens to create a festive tapestry that captures the essence of Spain. This day creates a lovely link between the holiday season and families' regular lives by embodying the spirit of what it means to be together, enjoy, and cherish one another.

The Epiphany celebrations bear witness to the love, togetherness, and tradition that characterize Spanish Navidad. The significance of this day is felt deeply with every parade, every meal eaten, and every laugh, reminding everyone that the true spirit of the holidays is not in the presents received but rather in the love and connection shared among family and friends. Whether you are a guest or a local taking part in the celebrations, Epiphany encapsulates the essence of Spanish culture, wrapping everyone in its colorful embrace and creating a memory that will reverberate for years to come.

CHAPTER 6
THE ART OF THE NATIVITY

The tradition of the nativity scene, or Belén, is the beating heart of Christmas in Spain. This exquisitely rendered portrayal of the birth of Jesus is much more than just a standard Christmas ornament; it captures the imagination and spirit of the occasion. Families all around the nation convert their houses, churches, and public spaces into small settings brimming with historical figures, picturesque settings, and narratives that link the past to the present. Every scene invites viewers to participate in the celebration of a cherished custom by presenting a distinct story that is brimming with color and life.

Making the Belén becomes a treasured family tradition in many Spanish homes. Usually, the scene opens with a carefully built cardboard or wood stable that serves as the backdrop for the Holy Family. The Three Wise Men, shepherds, angels, and other figures are added as the picture develops; each has a distinct role. Families gather around the dining table, reminiscing about former Belénes as they stitch together the complex intricacies of their new masterpiece. The nativity comes to life with stories passed down through the years, and children's creative additions make everyone laugh.

The regional diversity of the Belén is one noteworthy feature. For instance, artists in Andalusia are extremely proud of their work. Usually constructed of clay, the sculptures are painted in vibrant hues that give each character life. Some artists spend years honing their skills to the point when their studios resemble miniature galleries of nativity art. In some areas, whole communities may be made in little, depicting everyday activities and living in the surrounding environment. With the addition of these nuances, the Belén becomes a lively mosaic of customs and culture that captures not only the essence of Spanish life in general but also the story of the nativity.

These scenarios require a level of skill that goes beyond simple assembly. It's about establishing a connection to an enduring custom that keeps changing. Many families add contemporary touches to their Belénes to represent current affairs or regional traditions. Every scene is a distinct portrayal of the family's personality and values because of this fusion of the traditional and the modern. Each display honors the common heritage that unites the community while simultaneously celebrating uniqueness thanks to its creative design.

Public exhibits of Belénes appear in town squares and churches every December, bringing this joyous art form to the attention of both locals and tourists. Certain localities have contests when families and communities display their Belénes for the benefit of the community. When you stroll through these exhibits, you frequently come across expansive recreations that come with real creatures and striking backgrounds. These installations provide an engrossing and imaginative experience by immersing you in the heart of the nativity story.

The Belén custom originated in the Middle Ages and became well-known in Spain in the 18th century. It improves the entire Christmas season by acting as a visual reminder of the Christmas tale. Every element, from the meticulously constructed figures to the thoughtfully curated sceneries, contributes to telling a tale that strikes a deep chord in the Spanish psyche. The Belén invites everyone to consider the meaning of the season by encapsulating the essence of faith, hope, and community.

As the days of Advent spread, expectation increases. Families come together to uncover their Belén, which usually starts with the Baby Jesus—who usually doesn't appear until Christmas Eve—being placed. This uncomplicated gesture becomes into a treasured occasion, a custom that heralds the arrival of the festive season. Children eagerly look for the Baby Jesus figure in the days before Christmas, wanting to be the one to bring him into the scene. With everyone taking part in the celebration of their faith, this tradition provides an extra dimension of excitement and strengthens the family relationship.

Spanish Christmas parties likewise place a great emphasis on the nativity scene. The Belén is the focal point of the festivities during Nochebuena, the Christmas Eve family meal. Laughter and happiness abound as families enjoy their festive feast, and the nativity scene serves as a constant reminder of why they are all together. It promotes discussions on faith, customs, and the value of family. These exchanges weave the holiday's legacy into the fabric, fostering a sense of connection and belonging.

Many people turn visiting several Belénes during the holidays into a fun tradition in and of itself. Towns frequently host excursions that take visitors and residents alike to see the artistic and creative expressions found in different localities. Every visit offers fresh takes on the nativity tale that capture the soul and identity of the community. Families converse about the stories shown in each exhibit, and children eagerly point out their favorite characters and scenes. These outings generate enduring memories and are a lovely opportunity to discover the diverse facets of Spanish culture while commemorating the season.

The nativity scene's artistic quality carries over into music and performance. Villancicos, or traditional carols, are frequently performed in addition to the Belén, enhancing the experience even further. With their common melodies and lyrics, these songs span centuries as they tell the nativity tale. Reenactments of the nativity are a common component of community events in several areas, when people assemble to celebrate the birth of Jesus in a dynamic and interesting way. This fusion of narrative, music, and visual arts produces a lively ambiance that perfectly captures the spirit of the holidays.

Digital platforms and social media have started to affect how individuals interact with the Belén culture. Families post pictures of their works of art to encourage others to join in the celebration and to show off their inventiveness. People can connect via their enjoyment of this age-old custom, which creates a sense of community that transcends geographic borders thanks to this online engagement. Virtual displays of Belénes' artwork draw attention to the artistry involved and encourage others to continue the tradition and explore their own creativity.

Everyone is reminded of the value of family, community, and connection through the Belén tradition. It helps people feel like they belong during a time of year when hectic schedules and last-minute preparations are common. Engaging in the process of creating a nativity scene allows people to gain a greater appreciation for the meaning of Christmas. Each exhibit captures the artistry, inventiveness, and community spirit that make for a heartfelt reminder of the true spirit of the season.

Spanish Navidad is a special occasion to feel the coziness and happiness that come from participating in cherished customs. Beautifully capturing the essence of the season, the nativity scene's artwork celebrates faith, family, and culture. The Belén becomes a symbol of love and connection through shared experiences and artistic expression, beckoning everyone to partake in the celebration of life and hope. Long after the season is over, the stories conveyed by each character and setting remain, bringing back fond memories that never stop encouraging and inspiring.

The Belén—A Showcase of Craftsmanship

In Spain, the Belén is transformed into a colorful tableau that embodies Christmas, rather than just a straightforward nativity scene. Every display captivates everyone who sees it with its tale, reflecting heritage and exquisite craftsmanship. This yearly tradition spans decades, tying together a love of art, familial ties, and group happiness.

The Belén is a work of art in every detail. Many hours are spent by artisans crafting lifelike figures that capture the essence of the nativity. Every figure, from the pensive countenance of the Virgin Mary to the modest shepherds, narrates a distinct tale. Some have a rustic beauty that highlights the artisan's skill, while others come to life with vibrant colors and robes that seem to be caught in a light breeze. These characters' textures, colors, and stances all demonstrate a dedication to authenticity, bringing the Christmas story to life in homes, churches, and public spaces.

Families get together as the holidays draw near to put together their own Belén. Each member of the household participates, sharing memories and laughs as they arrange the figures, develop the landscape, and add personal touches. From grandparents to grandchildren, the procedure develops into a treasured custom that strengthens family bonds and produces enduring memories. Talks are easy as family members recall the special times they had spent together during past holidays and the backstories of each figurine.

Locations are another element that adds to Belén's appeal. Exquisite exhibits in public areas draw people from all over. While some have straightforward backgrounds, others have elaborate settings that show entire villages with hills, rivers, and small animals. Observers are drawn into a realm where Christmas enchantment is brought to life by these spectacular scenes. Local artists frequently exhibit their skill, putting years of effort and emotion into their creations. It's hard to ignore the tangible enthusiasm in the air as you stroll through these markets and take in the fine craftsmanship and intricacies on exhibit.

Different regions have different belén traditions, and each one adds a distinct flavor to the nativity scene. Figures may be dressed in traditional Andalusian garb in the southern regions, while the iconic caganer—a humorous figure crouching with pants down, a lighthearted addition that symbolizes fertility and good fortune—can be found in Catalonia. These regional variations help communities stay connected to their history while providing insights into the culture.

The Belén is generally the center of attention when families get together to celebrate. It turns into a space for introspection and a reminder of the principles and narratives that have shaped their life. With wide eyes, children approach, mesmerized by the minute details, the flashing lights, and the thoughtfully placed figures. Grandparents weave tales that have been passed down through the decades, and they listen closely as they tell the nativity narrative. Through this exchange, the family's understanding of their history is deepened and a bridge between the past and present is created.

In addition, local groups collaborate to produce expansive Belén displays. Through these cooperative initiatives, residents, artists, and volunteers are brought together to create immersive experiences in public areas. Every installation turns into a showcase for creativity and collaboration as people combine their skills to create something truly unique. Individuals from all backgrounds unite to make a contribution, be it through artistic aptitude, adeptness in managing tasks, or just providing a supportive hand. As a result, audiences are enthralled with a breathtaking show that simultaneously promotes a feeling of connection and belonging.

These installations attract a lot of visitors over the holidays, which livens up the festivities. Families are enjoying the sights and sounds, and the air is filled with the laughter and excitement of children and adults. Musicians often join the festivities, filling the ambiance with traditional carols, further enriching the experience. Every second spent with a Belén adds to the festive atmosphere by providing a window into Spain's rich cultural tapestry.

In this environment, the Belén appears as more than a decorative object. It turns into a dynamic representation of workmanship, culture, and ancestry. Communities are made proud of its traditions, which serve as a constant reminder to those involved that these practices must be preserved for the sake of future generations. The beauty and inventiveness that characterize Spanish culture are reflected in the excellent craftsmanship that goes into each figure and scenario. Beyond simply the nativity, it's a celebration of life, love, and community.

While many countries celebrate Christmas with trees, lights, and Santa Claus, the Belén stands as a particular icon of the season in Spain. Its exquisite workmanship and imaginative process serve as a reminder of the numerous customs that define the season. It promotes engagement and connection by inviting everyone to recognize the craftsmanship that goes into creating these tiny worlds.

The Belén, a symbol of the creative spirit and cultural values that pervade the festive season, emanates warmth and cheer in every corner of Spain, whether in busy cities or sleepy towns. A stunning tapestry of experiences is created when skill, custom, and group participation are combined, bringing people together for celebration and introspection.

Both people who create art and those who observe it are continually inspired by it. This unique feature of Spanish Christmas festivities encourages everyone to get into the spirit of the occasion, emphasizing the value of community, family, and the timeless beauty of craftsmanship. The Belén, with each figure expertly positioned and each detail executed, is a treasured representation of love and harmony that creates a deep emotional connection for everyone involved in this valued custom.

Live Nativity Scenes and Community Spirit

The smell of pine mixed with the warmth of freshly baked goods wafts across the streets as the lanterns flicker softly in the evening air. Throughout Spain, live nativity scenes are a beloved holiday tradition that come to life in towns and villages. Every year, towns unite to create magnificent renditions of the Nativity, converting public squares into enchanted depictions of that fateful night via the creative expression of their collective soul.

Families assemble to watch this dramatic reenactment of the birth of Christ, in which regional performers, frequently clad in the roles of Mary, Joseph, the shepherds, and even the wise men, bring the ancient tale to life. While some communities embrace a more rural character, with a modest stable nestled among bales of hay, others offer large shows with magnificent sets decked with glittering lights. Both inspire awe that knows no age limits, urging people to stop and consider the meaning of the season.

In many places, these scenes function as community-building initiatives that go beyond simple reenactments. Friends and neighbors band together and spend hours putting together sets, making costumes, and practicing lines. As the performance date draws near, there's a palpable thrill in the air that encourages teamwork and cooperation. Even the youngest residents of the neighborhood take part, excited to put on their costumes and assume parts that let them add to the custom. As families exchange tales and experiences, laughter reverberates through the streets, strengthening the community's bonds year after year.

The touching stories of local personalities typically give a special touch to the live nativity displays during the celebrations. Every representation has an own taste, with some communities including humor and customary folklore into the plays. Imagine the endearing antics of a cheeky sheep that wanders off and makes the audience chuckle, or a foolish donkey that playfully interrupts the scene's solemnity. People are connected by these carefree times, which evoke laughter and enduring memories long after the last show.

The dynamic spirit of these lively situations spreads throughout the neighborhood as visitors assemble to take in them. People congregate in the streets and mingle with the locals, who gladly share their customs and stories. Every performance encourages interaction and discourse amongst individuals from all walks of life in addition to bringing attention to the Nativity. Strangers connect over the thrill of seeing something genuinely amazing, smile warmly at each other, and exchange holiday pleasantries.

Communities frequently hold festive markets featuring artisan items, traditional meals, and seasonal treats in addition to live nativity scenes. The streets are occupied by vendors, whose stalls are filled to overflowing with handcrafted ornaments, treats like turrón, and aromatic spiced mulled wine. The sounds of live music, laughing, and conversation fill the air as local musicians perform traditional songs and carols, adding to the overall feeling of community.

Social gatherings are typically held during the evenings spent beneath the radiance of these real nativity displays. Families gather for substantial feasts, sharing foods rich in taste and history. Dinners feature locally inspired specialties that capture the essence of the season, such as rice flavored with saffron, roasted meats, and visually gorgeous yet delectable sweet pastries. These dinners are an opportunity to exchange warmth, humor, and stories, strengthening the ties that bind family and friends.

Live nativity displays have a certain enchantment that transcends the holiday season. Long after the last actors have taken their bows and the lights have gone down, the principles of love, solidarity, and community that are taught throughout these performances continue to be relevant. They provide people a feeling of direction and motivate them to act virtuously and compassionately every day.

The effect of these events is felt long after the Christmas lights go out. The people in the community who got together to put on the nativity scene now feel even closer, are motivated to work together on new initiatives, and are eager to preserve the sense of community that these customs create.

The spirit of these live nativity scenes develops over time into a treasured tradition that becomes woven into the very fabric of Spanish culture. New generations grow up participating in these events, bringing the stories forward and ensuring that the spirit of the season remains alive and well. The connections made by shared experiences, humor, and sincere dialogues are just as magical as the reenactments themselves.

These events transcend cultural barriers, inviting everyone to participate, see, and embrace the rich tapestry of life that distinguishes Spanish Navidad. The laughter, the stories, and the spirit of togetherness form a tapestry of experiences that continue to enrich the community year after year. The live nativity scenes capture the spirit of the season, bringing to light the ideals that unite people and fostering recollections that will last for future generations.

Ultimately, the allure of live nativity scenes is their capacity to bring people together in a celebration of tradition, faith, and community. These shows serve as a helpful reminder of the value of human connection and the happiness that results from exchanging experiences with individuals in our immediate vicinity. Communities all around Spain welcome the chance to gather together during the holidays, bringing love, laughter, and a strong feeling of community to their festivities.

SUMMARY

S pain's Christmas heartbeat is full of colorful energy, elaborate customs, and a sincere warmth that entices others to join in. This celebration is more than just one day; it expands like a beautifully wrapped gift, exposing layers of happiness, get-togethers with family, and mouthwatering feasts that leave a lasting impression. Every facet of the season, from lively markets to cozy family dinners, seems like a treasured memory just waiting to be created.

Madrid is a city that radiates joy during the holidays, with streets that are ablaze with bright lights and vibrant décor. With its wide selection of nativity figurines, handmade crafts, and sweet delicacies, the Mercado de Navidad in Plaza Mayor embodies the spirit of the holiday season and draws crowds. Every stall has a little of history to offer, and visitors are welcome to indulge in hot chocolate and crispy churros while embracing the infectious vibe of friendship and fun. This experience feels more like a community gathering than a simple shopping trip, mixing the ancient and contemporary in a tapestry of culture and joy.

Known as Nochebuena, Christmas Eve turns into a gourmet feast when families get together for the most important supper of the year. Tables brim with an abundance of delectable delicacies, with every mouthful recalling family customs and recipes handed down through the ages. Main courses include roasted lamb and seafood, which are enhanced by paella flavored with saffron and the delicious nougat known as turrón, which has been delighting palates since the Moorish era. A sense of solidarity is fostered by laughing and sharing stories around the table, where each dish narrates a unique tale of culture, history, and love.

An excitement surrounding the "El Gordo" lottery permeates the air as December 22 draws near. This lottery, popularly known as "the Fat One," enthralls the country and unites families as they assemble in front of televisions to cheer on their numbers. The pure joy of anticipation that unites communities, sparking discussions and forming relationships that last far beyond the holiday season, is more important than winning. An ordinary day becomes an incredible celebration of optimism and unity as the atmosphere fizzes with electricity.

Spain's celebrations culminate on January 5 with the magnificent parade known as the "Cabalgata de Reyes," which honors the advent of the Three Kings. Families are lining the streets, waiting for their children to toss sweets from brightly colored floats, and their eyes are sparkling with anticipation. The vivid spectacle draws together individuals from all walks of life, joined in mutual joy and anticipation. The night sky is illuminated with fireworks, a custom rich in culture and history that extends the festive spirit well into the new year.

Over the Christmas season, the "Belén" custom thrives. These painstakingly created nativity displays, which each tell a different story, adorn homes and public areas. While some prefer simplicity, others showcase entire communities, complete with miniature figures. Generations come together to celebrate the ingenuity and hard work that go into creating amazing displays, as each nativity scene provokes discussion. A sense of community is fostered by this mutual admiration, which invites everyone to embrace the spirit of the occasion.

Every meeting is surrounded by music, which permeates the atmosphere like a cozy blanket. Carols from the past fill homes, churches, and public spaces; impromptu performances unite neighbors. Street musicians frequently play tunes that entice onlookers to stop and savor the moment, fostering a happy mood that cuts beyond boundaries of language and culture. This feeling of community heightens the joyous mood and serves as a gentle reminder to everybody that Christmas is a shared experience rather than just a holiday.

Participation in a variety of community events is encouraged over the holidays, when people gather to share tales, laughter, and food. Everywhere you look, there's a spirit of unity that makes the holiday season feel like a group hug. Flamenco shows, exciting parties, and regional customs form a culturally rich atmosphere that invites everyone to participate in and add to the festive mood that permeates the streets.

Spanish Navidad takes on a distinct taste in every town and city, fusing regional traditions with universal themes of love and connection. The multiplicity of festivals observed throughout the regions highlights universally shared values while showcasing the beauty of diversity. Every celebration, whether it's a boisterous street festival or a calm evening spent with family, captures the spirit of tradition and community.

This time of year serves as a reminder of the value of friendship, family, and togetherness in addition to being a time for celebration. Every second spent together adds to the greater fabric of recollections that endure a lifetime. It's about spreading joy, enjoying the giving spirit, and establishing a welcoming atmosphere for all. This feeling of community deepens the meaning of the holidays and enhances the experience for both locals and guests.

Christmastime travel to Spain is a great way to get fully immersed in the culture. Every encounter offers a window into the essence of Spanish culture, from the bustling plazas teeming with music and laughter to the peaceful nooks where families congregate to swap tales. The joyful mood is complemented by the people's kindness, which invites everyone to take part in a celebration that knows no boundaries or customs.

In the end, the true meaning of Christmas in Spain is found in its capacity to bring people together by custom, cuisine, and shared memories. The holiday season offers as a reminder that every moment spent together is an opportunity to create memories, tell tales, and celebrate life. It creates a feeling of warmth and cheer that reverberates throughout the year, fostering a sense of connection that lasts long after the decorations are taken down.

The vibrant markets and joyous parades that characterize Spain's Christmas customs captivate the senses and evoke happiness. This time of year turns everyday experiences into unforgettable ones and invites everyone to join the colorful tapestry that is Spanish Navidad. Adopting these customs reveals the beauty of community and connection at the core of the holiday season, allowing for a deeper knowledge of the cultural subtleties that make this celebration so unique.

Don't miss out!

Visit the website below and you can sign up to receive emails whenever Stacy Mills publishes a new book. There's no charge and no obligation.

https://books2read.com/r/B-A-DTPKC-CVKBF

Connecting independent readers to independent writers.

Did you love *Christmas in Spain : How to Enjoy a Traditional Spanish Navidad*? Then you should read *The Smart Holiday Planner : Budgeting for a Merry Christmas*[1] by Stacy Mills!

[2]

The holidays are right around the corner, and if you're anything like the 65% of Americans who overspend during this festive season, it's time to turn things around. Imagine ringing in the New Year without the anxiety of mounting credit card debt and financial regrets. Picture a holiday season where joy and generosity come without the sting of a budget hangover. You don't need a magic wand to make it happen—just a smart plan.

Recent research reveals that the average American family plans to spend around $1,200 this year on holiday gifts, decorations, and festivities. That's a hefty chunk of change, especially when you consider that 40% of people are still paying off last year's holiday bills come spring. Don't let yourself fall into the same trap. Instead, arm yourself with the right tools to ensure your holiday cheer doesn't come at the cost of your financial peace of mind.

---

1. https://books2read.com/u/4j7gk2

2. https://books2read.com/u/4j7gk2

This guide provides straightforward strategies and practical tips to keep your holiday spending in check while maximizing the fun and festivities. No need for jargon or complex formulas—just clear, actionable advice to help you enjoy the season without the financial fallout. From tracking expenses and setting realistic budgets to finding creative ways to save, every page is packed with information designed to simplify your holiday planning and keep your wallet happy.

The average holiday shopper's credit card balance grows by 25% during the season, but you can break this cycle. Learn how to use holiday sales to your advantage, craft a budget that actually works, and make savvy choices about where and how you spend your money. It's all about smart decisions and savvy planning, and this guide equips you with everything you need to get it right.

But it's not just about numbers and spreadsheets. This book also guides you through the emotional side of budgeting, helping you to enjoy the holiday spirit without sacrificing the things that matter most. Get inspired to create memorable experiences that don't break the bank. Discover how to find joy in the small things and how thoughtful planning can lead to an unforgettable holiday season.

Why should you spend hours stressing over your budget when you could be enjoying quality time with loved ones? This book helps you strike the perfect balance between celebration and financial responsibility, ensuring that your holidays are filled with cheer rather than stress. Say goodbye to the guilt and anxiety of overspending and hello to a season where you can truly enjoy every moment.

The end of the year is a time for reflection and new beginnings. Use this opportunity to transform your holiday habits and start the new year off right. No more surprises, no more debt—just the joy of a well-planned and well-loved holiday season. This guide is your go-to resource for making the most of your festive season while keeping your budget on track. Get ready to plan smarter, spend wisely, and celebrate like never before.

Also by Stacy Mills

The Strategic Christmas Planner : Christmas Made Simple
Christmas in San Francisco : Love, Magic, and Miracles by the Bay
The Christmas Vegetarian : A Vegetarian's Guide to a Meat Free Christmas
Christmas Cash Flow : Proven Strategies for Holiday Financial Success
Noel in Germany : How to Celebrate the Holidays like a True Local
The Smart Holiday Planner : Budgeting for a Merry Christmas
German Christmas Shopping : A Shopper's Wonderland
Christmas in Spain : How to Enjoy a Traditional Spanish Navidad